Introduct

This book ... by St. Elizabeth Ann Seton, like the previous volume, *Hope Always Awake* (2017), was published for the greater glory of God and to spread awareness of the spiritual wisdom of the first native-born American to be declared a saint. The title comes from a letter Mother Seton wrote to a friend recounting her decision to enter the Catholic Church.

St. Elizabeth's decision to enter the Catholic Church came only after a long and painful personal struggle. And, as her words profess, it meant surrendering to God her security, her future and her heart. The Lord abundantly blessed Mother Seton for her surrender and through her and the Daughters and Sisters of Charity who continue the mission of their foundress, He continues to bless the Church universal.

I hope these reflections and prayers will help others to surrender their lives into the hands of our loving God. They are arranged alphabetically by the first word of each quote. There is also an index by subject in the back of the booklet.

I am grateful to Regina Bechtle, S.C. and Judith Metz, S.C. for their friendship and their assistance with this project. The quotations contained in this booklet were compiled from Mother Seton's writings published in *Elizabeth Bayley Seton: Collected Writings Volumes I – IIIB,* edited by Sr. Regina and Sr. Judith. These volumes are available online at http://via.library.depaul.edu/vincentian_ebooks. The texts in brackets attached to some quotes were added for purposes of clarity. They are not Mother Seton's actual words.

I am also very grateful to the Daughters of Charity of St. Joseph's House in Emmitsburg for their kindness and hospitality.

Fr. Rory T. Conley

September 2019

Emmitsburg, Maryland

St. Elizabeth Ann Seton was born in New York City in 1774 of English and French ancestry. Elizabeth's mother died when she was only three years old and due to the frequent absences of her father, Dr. Richard Bayley, she was largely raised by relatives. Elizabeth was brought up as a devout Episcopalian and from her earliest years was dedicated to reading the Bible. After a brief engagement, Elizabeth married William Magee Seton in January 1794. Their marriage was a happy one, and they had five children, Anna, William, Richard, Catherine and Rebecca. However, in part due to the economic disruptions caused by the Napoleonic wars in Europe, William Seton's mercantile business went bankrupt in 1801. The once well-to-do family was thrust into impoverishment. Additionally, William Seton contracted tuberculosis. In a desperate attempt to restore his health in a warmer climate, the young couple and their daughter Anna went to Italy in the fall of 1803. But William did not recover and died in Italy less than two months after their arrival.

Elizabeth and Anna were taken in by her husband's friends, the Filicchis, who were devout Catholics. Forced by circumstances to remain with the Filicchi family for five months, Elizabeth was drawn to Catholicism, particularly to belief in the Real Presence of Jesus in the Holy Eucharist. Upon her return to the United States in April 1804, Elizabeth's desire to convert to Catholicism was stifled by the opposition of some in her family who threatened to cut off all their support to the young widow and her five children. Faced with her family's opposition, Elizabeth struggled for almost a year with her decision to convert to Catholicism. But finally, in spite of the very real threat of destitution, Elizabeth was received into the Catholic Church and made her first Holy Communion on March 25, 1805.

Following her conversion, Elizabeth labored to provide for her family by operating a small school. However, anti-Catholic sentiment in New York was very strong at that time and she was forced to close the school due to a lack of students. Through the intervention of Catholic clergy, most importantly Bishop John Carroll, Elizabeth Ann Seton was able to establish a successful school in Baltimore in 1808. It was there that under the guidance of the Holy Spirit that Elizabeth Ann Seton was led to establish an order of religious women in America. With the support of Bishop Carroll, Elizabeth made her vows as a religious sister on the Feast of the Annunciation, March 25,

1809. Confident that Elizabeth Ann Seton would be the spiritual leader of other women religious, Bishop John Carroll began calling her "Mother Seton." Mother Seton's new community, the Sisters of Charity of St. Joseph, adopted the rule of life of the Daughters of Charity established by St. Vincent DePaul in France in 1633. As she still embraced her primary calling as a mother to her own children, the challenges that St. Elizabeth Ann faced as a religious founder were enormous.

Through the generosity of a benefactor, Mother Seton was given a large farm in Emmitsburg, Maryland, on which to establish her new religious community and a school for girls. The band of sisters arrived in Emmitsburg in June 1809 and opened their school, St. Joseph's Academy, in February 1810. The school that Mother Seton and her sisters established was open to needy students as well as to those who could pay. It was one of the very first Catholic schools in the United States and for this reason Mother Seton is the patron saint of our Catholic schools.

The Sisters of Charity experienced rapid growth and over the next dozen years, eighty-six women entered the community at Emmitsburg. The new community also experienced many hardships as a result of lack of funds, primitive living conditions and disease. Eighteen of the first Sisters of Charity died in the first twelve years of the community's existence. More difficult still for Mother Seton were the deaths of her daughters, Anna and Rebecca, and her beloved sisters-in-law, Harriet and Cecelia.

Not long after the establishment of the foundation in Emmitsburg, bishops throughout the country began requesting the services of Mother Seton's sisters. In 1814, they were asked to take over the operation of an orphanage in Philadelphia. In 1817 they established the Roman Catholic Orphan Asylum in New York. Additional foundations followed soon after but Mother Seton did not live to see them.

On January 4, 1821, worn out from the struggles of a hard but fruitful life, Elizabeth Ann Seton died at the age of forty-seven. Fittingly, in 1975, Elizabeth Ann Bayley Seton was officially proclaimed a saint on September 14, the Feast of the Triumph of the Cross. She was the first native-born American to be declared a saint.

Through the years of planting her community and fostering its growth, Mother Seton was dedicated to maintaining regular correspondence with a diverse group of relatives, friends, clergy and laity. For many of them she was a spiritual guide. It is largely in her letters, extracts of which are published here, that Mother Seton's spiritual wisdom is to be found.

Rev. Rory T. Conley, Ph. D.

Source: "St. Elizabeth Ann Bayley Seton"
by Sr. Betty Ann McNeil, D.C.
New Catholic Encyclopdia (2003).

1. A true joy to me indeed the daily morning Sacrifice and our frequent, and daily communion when prepared. What a contrast to the morning sleep in former days. It has been my wealth in poverty, and joy in deepest afflictions. CW II, 489.

2. Above all blessings I adore Thy infinite goodness that vouchsafes to regard the sorrows of a child of the dust. All nature is bright, every blessing below is perfect, but my Heart is hot within me, at the feet of my Saviour I fall. Through His adored Holy Name I look to You for help-All Glory be to You who gives me the saving help-All GLORY be to Him who suffered to save us. All glory be to the Sanctifying Gift of His love which enables us to approach You and tho[ugh] disobedient, unworthy, wretched creatures, yet permits us to call to our Father, Redeemer, and Comforter. CW IIIa, 33.

3. Adored Lord, increase my faith — perfect it — crown it Your own. Your choicest, dearest Gift, having drawn me from the pit and borne me to Your fold, keep me in Your sweet pastures — and lead me to eternal life. Amen. Amen. Amen. CW I, 479.

4. Again, and again this poor heart is offered in every way He will make use of it. CW II, 3.

5. All in our God, whether cloudy or clear, that is our comfort   the world or anything in it can neither give or take. CW II, 526.

6. All nature speaks to us of heave — the delights of the morning — a flower of the field. CW IIIa, 250.

7. All things here only for His glory. CW II, 590.

8. Almighty Giver of all Mercies, Father of all, who knows my heart and pities its weakness and errors. You know the desire of my soul is to do Your will. It struggles to wing its flight to You, its creator, and sinks again in sorrow for that imperfection which draws it back to earth. CW IIIa, 36.

9. Alone on a rock this afternoon, surrounded by the most beautiful scenery, adoring and praising Him for his magnificence and glory, the heavy eye could find no delight; the soul cried out, "0 God! 0 God! Give yourself. What is all the rest?" A silent voice of love answered, "I am yours." "Then, dearest Lord! keep me as I am while I live; for this is true content - to hope

for nothing, to desire nothing, expect nothing, fear nothing. Death! Eternity! Oh, how small are all objects of busy, striving, restless, blind, mistaken beings, when at the foot of the cross these two prospects are viewed! CW II, 707.

10. Arrest, O merciful Father, the soul that flees from You or is insensible to Your mercies; draw it by Your powerful grace; awaken it by Your subduing Spirit, that convinced of its infirmities and bewailing its unworthiness, it may throw itself on Your mercy and find pardon and peace through the merits of our adored Savior. CW IIIa, 25.

11. As birds in changing their places find the air wherever they fly, and fish who live in the water are surrounded by their element wherever they swim, so wherever we go, we must find God everywhere. He is more within us, than we are in ourselves. CW IIIa, 392.

12. As Sisters of Charity we should fear nothing. CW II, 90

13. At all events, happen now what will, I rest with GOD – the tabernacle and Communion – so now I can pass the Valley of Death itself. CW I, 378

14. At last GOD IS MINE and I AM HIS. Now let all go its round. I HAVE RECEIVED HIM. CW I, 376.

15. Be but faithful to Him with your whole heart, and never fear. He will support, direct, console, and finally crown your dearest Hope. Leave all to Him. All you have to do is pray. CW I, 539

16. Beloved child of Jesus, you shall have the victory, and He the glory. To Him be glory forever who has called you to so glorious a combat, and so tenderly supports you through it. You will triumph, for it is Jesus who fights, not you my dear one. CW II, 21.

17. Blessed be my precious Shepherd in this last hour of His day. I am at rest within His fold sweetly refreshed with the waters of comfort. Glory to my God for this unspeakable blessing. CW IIIa, 23.

18. Blessed vocation, blessed they who understand. When our Jesus said the beatitudes, what did He mean, the momentary blessing for the earth? O no, He blessed indeed for heaven where He shall wipe all tears from every eye. No more sorrow or sighing, endless love and

harmony, the Song of Mary, her voice of praise.
CW IIIa, 314.

19. By this most holy sacrifice, pity me, my Lord. It is the only offering I can worthily make. It is my all, since it is Yourself my Jesus, my victim of sin, my redemption, my cleansing and reconciliation; My JESUS who paid for me in the manger, was nailed for me to the cross, bleeding and dying for me, saying for me [to] His Father "Father forgive," and to his Mother "Behold your child". CW IIIa, 269.

20. Cheerfulness prepares a generous mind for all the noblest acts of religion — love, adoration, praise, and every union with our God. CW, IIIb, 31.

21. Come then, O death! That I may no more offend my God, no more oppose His will. Come take my soul, deliver it from this wretched frailty which makes it fall so often, and for what is, in itself, nothing. Come, I do desire You, desire You with my whole heart.
CW IIIa, 416.

22. Come, my Jesus, my only hope, since You condescend to come to me, I go out to meet You as my King and my God. O sweet condescension of my Lord...what is my hope and desire but to be united to You! How can my desires refrain to meet those of my God, my Savior, my King, only desirable indeed, and beautiful above all. So lovely in Himself, but unspeakably beautiful and good to me. Can desires fall short, can I remain insensible to my God — to the supreme, the incomprehensible honor and happiness He offers me? No, no my Jesus! CW IIIa, 273.

23. Considering [that] through faith and hope in the merits of our Divine Redeemer, we are His children and the purchase of His blood, we more naturally anticipate with joy that which will deliver us. CW I, 545.

24. Courage, dearest child of Eternity – Be Faithful. CW II, 513.

25. Dear Darling Child, your peace is from God. It is the sweet reward He has promised to His children. Docile to His commands and fervent in their love, their very sacrifices become their pleasures, being accompanied by the

conscious joy of pleasing Him [whom] they love above all. CW I, 409

26. [It was a] delight to sit alone by the water side — wandering hours on the shore, humming and gathering shells — every little leaf and flower or animal, insect, shades of clouds, or waving trees, objects of thoughts of God and heaven. CW IIIa, 511.

27. Do I realize it? The protecting presence, the consoling grace of my Redeemer and God. He raises me from the dust to feel that I am near Him. He drives away all sorrow to fill me with His consolations. He is my guide, my friend and supporter — With such a guide can I fear? With such a friend, should I not be satisfied? With such a supporter can I fall? Oh! Then, my adored refuge, let not my frail nature shrink at Your command. Let not the spirit, which You vouchsafest [granted] to fill, reluctantly obey You. Rather, let me say, Lord, here am I, the creature of Your will, rejoicing that You will lead, thankful that You will choose for me. Only continue to [grant] me Your soul- cheering presence. And in life or in death, let me be Your own. CW IIIa, 32.

28. Do we remember that we are sinners and as sinners we suffer, and even be thankful for occasions to redeem the past? Do we consecrate ourselves to God as our All in all with the true service of the heart? CW III, 331.

29. And our charity, does it extend to all? Is our love for all in our Jesus? Is our whole heart truly His? Do we unite it so closely with Him that life – soul and body – are all devoted to Him? With Saint Francis, do we seek if there is the smallest hidden fiber of that heart not His, to tear it out and break its root? And with Saint Paul, can we say we are hidden with Him in God; that Jesus lives in us; that we are a part of His body and as the beating of the heart sends the blood to every part of His body to nourish it, does the life of our Jesus animate us? Do we indeed give Him the true service of heart without which whatever else we give has no value? CW IIIa,332.

30. [Do all our] exercises in the Spirit of HUMILITY, SIMPLICITY, and CHARITY, in union with those our Lord did when on earth. CW IIIb, 280.

31. Eternity, oh how near it often seems to me. Think of it when you are hard pushed. How long will be that day without a night, or that night without a day. May we praise and bless and adore forever. ASJPH, XII, B14 August 20, 1818. Dirvin 33

32. Eternity — in what light shall we view [things], if we think of such trifles in the company of God and the choirs of [the] Blessed. What will we think of the trials and cares, pains and sorrows we had once upon earth? Oh, what a mere nothing! Let then they who weep be as though they wept not, they who rejoice as though they rejoice not, they who obtain as though they possess not. This world passes away. Eternity! that voice to be everywhere understood. Eternity! to love and serve Him only who is to be loved and eternally served and praised in Heaven. CW IIIa, 523.

33. Every day of life more and more increases my gratitude to God for having made me what I am. CW II, 488.

34. Every morning at the Divine Sacrifice I offer... the whole success to Him whose blessed will alone can sanctify and make it fruitful. CW II, 28.

35. Faith, faith my dear friend! the Captain marches on. Oh, yes, we follow, we follow. CW II, 708.

36. Father Almighty, I know not what I would ask or how to give words to the desires of my soul. But this I know, it is You I would seek and You know every desire and wish that is there. For this, above all blessings, I adore Your infinite goodness that vouchsafes [grants] to regard the sorrows of a child of the dust. CW IIIa, 33.

37. Fear not, the love which nourishes us is unchangeable as Him from whom it proceeds. CW IIIb, 2.

38. For my part, I try to make my very breathing a continual Thanksgiving. CW II, 643.

39. For is He not the God of our affairs? Do they not all belong to him? Is He not our God in our labors as well as in our rest? And when do we need His light and assistance more than when we are in difficulty or confusion? CW IIIa, 406.

40. For us to have such an offering, our own Savior and Redeemer, who seeing we had nothing we could offer but our poverty and misery, came Himself to be made our own victim, of praise and love in the manger, on the cross, in the blessed sacrifice of our altars, and in the sacred Holy Communion for which we now prepare- our Jesus, our compassionate Savior, oh prepare us indeed! CW IIIa, 268.

41. Give me, O my God, this patient and unalterable charity – this beneficent charity which refuses nothing; this universal charity which excepts [withholds] nothing... O my God, if indeed I love You, how can I not love those that You identify with Yourself? Are they not my brethren [brothers and sisters]? Do I not love You in loving them? What I do for them, is it not done for You? Surely this consideration is enough to soften the most insensible heart. CW IIIa, 193.

42. Go to Him, tell Him you are in want of everything, beg for the new heart, the right spirit, and that He will teach you to do the things that please Him. CW I, 337.

43. God fills us with His mercies which are new every morning. He covers us with His wings, carries us on His shoulders and cherishes us as a mother nurses the child of her bosom. CW IIIa, 392.

44. God is always near those who labor for His glory. We have nothing to fear. CW IIIa, 434.

45. God Is Mine and I Am His — Now let all go its round — I Have Received Him. CW I, 376.

46. God sees each one of us as precisely as if we were alone in the wide universe. What a deep thought – that God Himself is the very life of our being, that He dwells in the soul of each one of us as in His own element! CW IIIa, 395.

47. God will be a faithful God to you, if you are faithful to Him. CW II, 518.

48. God would surely refuse nothing to His Mother, and she could not help loving and pitying the poor souls He died for... In the Blessed Virgin Mary I felt really I had a Mother, which You know, my foolish heart so often laments to have lost in early days. From the first remembrance of infancy, I have looked in all the plays of

childhood and wildness of youth, to the clouds for my Mother. And at that moment it seemed as if I had found more than her, even [the] tenderness and pity of a Mother. So I cried myself to sleep in her heart. CW I, 293.

49. Hard as separation from dear ones is, I know it must be submitted to, and of course, look up with hope is all I can do. CW II, 611.

50. Have confidence, never let the comparison of time and Eternity slip a moment from your mind. I find that this cures all sorrow. CW, 680.

51. He, who sits above, smiles at the anxious, calculating heart, and makes everything easy to the simple and confiding. CW I, 435.

52. He gives us every grace. This grace is able to carry us through every obstacle and difficulty. CW IIIa, 262.

53. He is my guide, my friend and supporter. With such a guide, can I fear? With such a friend, shall I not be satisfied? With such a supporter can I fall? CW IIIa, 32.

54. He who lives in my heart never suffers me to forget that the seed I am now sowing you in tears, shall certainly be reaped in joy, and this certainty is so ever present with me and bears me up so lightly over the briars and thorns that I often stop in the midst of hurry and beg my dear Savior to assure me that it is not temptation, and that He will not let my enemy persuade me there is peace when there is no peace. He always answers "Do not fear, while your peace is in Me alone it cannot be false." CW I, 387.

55. He who perseveres to the end shall be saved. Piety must be habitual, not by fits. It must be persevering because temptations continue all our life and perseverance alone obtains the crown. Its means are [awareness of] the presence of God, good reading, prayer, the sacraments, good resolutions often renewed, the remembrance of our last ends. Its advantages — habits which secure our predestination, making our life equal [balanced], peaceable, and consoling, leading to the heavenly crown where our perseverance will be eternal!!! CW IIIb, 12.

56. He will direct your heart to that prayer of the Spirit which neither occupations nor pain can drive from it – though it may not be active, still it is there. CW III, 527.

57. Heaven cannot separate You from Your children; nor can earth detain them from You. Raise us up by a life of faith in You. CW IIIa, 25.

58. Here my God I go, said I, heart all to You. CW I, 374.

59. His Apostles without learning, education or intelligence, often were unable to comprehend His instructions, obliging Him to repeat and re-explain the same things. Often too, they required His mediation in their dissensions. Living with them and conversing with them, He always remained patient. CW IIIa, 194.

60. His will forever, in the smallest as well as in the greatest thing. I know you say, Amen. CW II, 242.

61. His will, which if we make a right use of it, is always for our true happiness, must take [the] place of all. And we by patiently submitting, will obtain His dear love which is worth every other possible blessing. CW I, 542.

62. Hope, always awake, whispers Mercy for the future, as sure as the past. CW I, 445.

63. Hope must go on with us, for it will not do for hearts and fortunes to sink together. CW I, 107.

64. How happy should we be if our eyes were open to this truth — If we saw by faith, with the eyes of our soul, everywhere, within and without us, the three Persons of the adorable Trinity with their divine attributes, what would be the dangers and events of this life be to us in His presence to whom earth and hell are subjected? CW IIIa,393.

65. How He loves and welcomes the poor and desolate. CW IIIb, 34.

66. How many ways there are indeed of proving my love to You my Jesus. All the day long, with the blessed morning sacrifices, I may send up my acts of adoration, faith, hope and love, of sorrow for my sins and desires for Your blessings on all my preparations of duty and love through the day. CW IIIa, 268.

67. Human passions and weaknesses are never extinct, but they cannot triumph in the heart which is possessed by peace. CW II, 86.

68. I am a prisoner too — with all this wide and beautiful creation before me, the restless soul longs to enjoy its liberty and rest beyond its bound. When the Father calls His child — how readily He will be obeyed! CW 157.

69. I am ashamed, O Lord, to come to You, even to thank You for Your mercy. Your mercy in so long having patience with my repeated sins and disobedience to Your holy word. But whatever I am, though so miserable and hateful even to my guilty self, Your attributes can never change. Your goodness and Your mercy know no bounds. CW I, 303.

70. I am going straight on by faith. CW II, 78.

71. I am the happiest creature in the thought that not the least thing can happen but by His will or permission, and all for the best. CW II, 373.

72. I can only say I do long and desire to worship our God in truth. CW I, 371.

73. I carry you constantly in my heart before Him who loved us, and so much more than any friend can love a friend. May He bless you, strengthen you, and make you truly pleasing to Him, own dear friend of my heart. CW II, 492.

74. I desire to receive You, my Savior, with unspeakable desire, but O cover first my whole soul with Your blood. My sins must be first cleansed in it before Your heavenly visit; cleanse me more and more, then seal me for Your own to everlasting life. CW IIIa, 273.

75. I do truly grieve at what grieves you, beloved friend, to see our poor Protestant friends doubly blinded by the miserable conduct of Catholics, but so it ever was. CW II, 622.

76. I feel an inexpressible resentment against its [the world's] barbarous laws. CW II, 560.

77. I find invariably that when I leave all absolutely to Him, He either bestows what is desired, or grants so much consolation that all is peace. CW II, 230.

78. I have always found when under any particular trial of patience, a great consolation in the Litany of our Blessed Mother. After renewing promises to our dear Lord, which we know we have often broken, and fear to break again, it is sweet to entreat her who bore Him in her bosom of peace to take our case in hand. If she is not heard, who shall be? CW I, 442.

79. I have been in a sea of troubles.... But the guiding star is always bright, and the Master of the storm always in view. CW I, 414.

80. I have been to what is called here among so many churches the Catholic Church. When I turned the corner of the street it is in, "Here, my God, I go," said I, "heart all to You." Entering it, how that heart died away, as it were, in silence before the little tabernacle and the great crucifixion over it. — Ah, my God, here let me rest," said I. CW I, 375.

81. I have had a great many, very hard trials. This fire of tribulation is no doubt meant to consume the many imperfections and bad dispositions our Lord finds in me. Indeed, it has at times burnt so deep that the anguish could not be

concealed. But, by degrees, custom reconciles pain itself, and I determine, dry and hard as my daily bread is, to take it with as good grace as possible. When I carry it before our Lord sometimes He makes me laugh at myself and asks me what other kind I would choose in the valley of tears than that which Himself and all His followers made use of. CW II, 92.

82. I hope to meet you triumphant over all the obstacles to your happy eternity – Bless you forever. CW II, 505.

83. I know very well He sees differently from man, and as obedience is His favorite service and cannot lead me wrong, according to the old rule, I look neither behind nor before, but straight upwards without thinking of human calculations. CW I, 432.

84. I long and wish to serve our Lord with every breath I draw. CW II, 129.

85. I look to the far, so far distant shore, the heaven of heavens. A few days more and Eternity. Now then, all resignation, love, abandon. Rest in Him — the heart in sweet bitterness. CW IIIa, 432.

86. I must jog on the allotted path through all its windings and weariness till it brings me home, where all tears shall be wiped away and sorrow and sighing be heard no more. In the meanwhile... courage, LOOK UP! CW I, 345.

87. I need not tell you to rise above the clouds that surround us. You know well enough that we must pass our course of trials with the rest of human beings. CW II, 473.

88. I often think my sins, my miseries, hide the light. Yet I will cling and hold to my God to the last gasp, begging for that light and never change until I find it. CW I, 368.

89. [I] received the longing desire of my soul. Merciful Lord! What a privilege! May we never, never leave the sheltering wing, but dwelling now under the shadow of His Cross, we will cheerfully gather the thorns which will be turned hereafter into a joyful crown. CW I, 473.

90. I repeat, these are my happiest days. Sometimes the harassed mind, wearied with continual contradiction to all it would most covet – solitude, silence, peace – sighs for a change.

But five minutes of recollection procures an immediate act of resignation, convinced that this is the day of salvation for me. And if like a coward, I should run away from the field of battle, I am sure the very peace I seek would fly from me, and the state of penance sanctified by the will of God would be again wished for as the safest, surest road. CW I, 444.

91. I see all in the order of Providence. CW II, 642.

92. I see the everlasting hills so near, and the door of my Eternity so wide open that I turn too wild sometimes. CW II, 606.

93. I shall be free bye and bye, and able to go in my turn without one string to pull me back. CW II, 449.

94. I thought at that time my father did not care for me. Well, God was my Father, my all. I prayed — sung hymns— cried — laughed in talking to myself of how far He could place me above all sorrow, then laid still to enjoy the heavenly peace that came over my soul. CW I, 264.

95. I will go peaceably and firmly to the Catholic Church. For if faith is so important to our salvation, I will seek it where true faith first began, seek it among those who received it from God Himself. The controversies on it I am quite incapable of deciding, and as the strictest Protestant allows salvation to a good Catholic, to the Catholics I will go, and try to be a good one. May God accept my intention and pity me. CW I, 374.

96. I will tell you the plain truth, that my habits both of soul and body are changed, and that I feel all the habits of society and connections of this life have taken a new form and are only interesting or endearing as they point the view to the next. CW I, 212.

97. "If anyone loves Me, he will keep my commandments," (Jn 14:15). These also are Your own words, my adorable Savior, and I know from them I must prove my love to You by my fidelity. CW IIIa, 268.

98. If I get through my task with the sacrifice of the most incessant care and attention, and in the end feel the satisfaction of having performed

it well, it is as much as I can expect, and more than I dare to hope. To intend the best and be thankful for the present, is the only plan I can resolve on. CW I, 48.

99. If the holy Scriptures say so much of judgment, they are also filled with sentences for heaven — St. Peter, St. Paul, St. John in the Apocalypse, the very last word the Spirit says — Come —, we answer — Lord Jesus, Come quickly! CW IIIa, 313.

100. If we did not now know and love God — If we did not feel the consolations, and embrace the cheering hope He has set before us, and find our delight in the study of His blessed word and truth, what would become of us? CW I, 259.

101. INFINITE LOVE INFINITE GOODNESS multiplied and applied by OMNIPOTENCE is enough FOR His little worm to make it smile and rejoice even on His calvary where it nailed Him to show such wonders. OH BLESSED BLESSED BLESSED WHAT INDEED IS LIFE, I AM CRAZY. CW II, 664.

102. In [the] place of your retirement [quiet] be alone with Your conscience. Turn your heart toward God to entreat Him with sincerity to assist you, that You may discover all Your faults. But do not trouble and torment your mind. Examine yourself seriously, diligently, with a sincere desire to know and confess your sins. But after that, be at rest ... God, Who sees the bottom of your heart and the sincerity of your intention and endeavors, will forgive them. CW IIIa, 383.

103. In the hour of manifestation when all this cross-working will be explained, we will find that in this period of our poor life, we are most ripe for the business for which we were sent. While the ploughers go over us, then we are safe. No fears of pleasing ourselves, no danger of mistaking God's will. CW II, 706.

104. Is it nothing to sleep serene under His guardian wing? To awake to the brightness of the glorious sun with renewed strength and renewed blessings? – to be blessed with the power of instant communion with the Father of our spirits, the sense of His presence and the power of His love? To be assured

of that love is enough to tie us faithfully to Him and while we have fidelity to Him all the surrounding cares and contradictions of this life are but cords of mercy to bind us more strongly to Him who will hereafter make even their remembrances vanish in the reality of our eternal felicity [happiness]. CW IIIa, 24.

105. Is there now anything so dear to us as hope... Heavenly hope. Cherish it... and it will carry us through triumphant. CW I, 494.

106. It has been the Lord's day, indeed to me although many, many temptations to forget my heavenly possession in His constant presence have pressed upon me. But blessed be my precious Shepherd in this last hour of His day. I am at rest within His fold, sweetly refreshed with the waters of comfort which have flowed through the soul of His ministering servant, our Blessed Teacher. Glory to God for these unspeakable blessings! Glory to my God for the means of grace and the hopes of glory which He so mercifully bestows on His unworthy servant. CW IIIa, 23.

107. It is a sweet thought to dwell on, that those I most tenderly love, love God; and if we do not meet again here, there we shall be separated no more. APSJH, XVII, 14 Dirvin p.28

108. It is sweet to entreat her, who bore Him in her bosom of peace, to take our own case in hand. If she is not heard, who shall be? CW I, 442.

109. It is true the journey is long, the burden is heavy. But the Lord delivers His faithful servants from all their troubles – and sometimes even here allows them some hours of sweetest peace. CW IIIa, 24.

110. It would be ungrateful in [of] me after all our God has done for me and mine to be discouraged now, distrusting His future goodness. CW II, 468.

111. Jesus on the breast of Mary feeding on her milk. How long she must have delayed the weaning of such a child! How happy the earth to possess her so long – a secret blessing to the rising Church. The Blessed Trinity could not part so soon with the perfect praise arising from the earth as long as she remained. How

darkened in the sight of angels when she was removed from it. CW IIIb, 19.

112. Hasten, hasten, happy moment! Time, I bid you fly. Awaken me to eternity, and bid this body die. CW IIIb, 108.

113 Keep in mind that not the least thing can happen to you without the will of God with regard to you.... Deposit then in the heart of your Savior all your pains. Beg Him to give you a heart so conformed to His own that you may receive every cross as from the hand of His Father, that you may desire only what He desired, love only what He loved, and seek only what He sought, which was the will of His Father every moment of his life. CW IIIa, 526.

114. Keep your heart high with mine. Our God will turn all right for us, if only you will be faithful to him. CW II, 417.

115. Let me kiss the path of Mount Calvary sprinkled with Your blood since it is that path alone which leads me to You. CW IIIb, 77.

116. Let, indeed, Your coming be present to me in all my thoughts and actions. Strengthen me to overcome, for Your sake, every weakness — poor nature experiences in my daily tasks of duty — that every hour may be sanctified in the spirit of preparation for Your blessed visit so near, and all my actions done with pure desires and faithful intentions. CW III, 268.

117. Let that one mercy of our God lighten all your pains, my beloved child — Oh that I could take them, but I can only carry them to our All in my poor heart that loves you dearly. CW II, 587.

118. Let us humbly beg with the poor man in the Gospel, Lord grant that I may see — for though we see not, yet where can we go from His Spirit? Where can we hide from His presence? As the Psalmist expresses, neither heaven or hell, or the uttermost parts of the sea can cover us from Him. As birds in changing their places find the air wherever they fly, and fish who live in the water are surrounded by their element wherever they swim, so wherever we go, we must find God everywhere. He is more within us, than we are in ourselves. CW IIIa, 392.

119. Let us always whisper His Name of Love as the antidote to all discord that surrounds us... the harmony of heaven begins to us while silent from all the world, we again and again repeat it — Jesus, Jesus, Jesus, Jesus. CW I, 478.

120. Link by link, the blessed chain, One Body in Christ —He the head, we the members. One Spirit diffused through the Holy Spirit in us all. One Hope —Him in heaven and Eternity. One Faith —by His Word and His Church. One Baptism and participation of [in] His sacraments. One God —our dear Lord. One Father — we His children. He above all, through all and in all. CW IIIb, 108.

121. Look up my soul, fear not, the love which nourishes us is as unchangeable as Him from whom it proceeds. It will remain when every other sentiment will vanish. And could we desire more than to draw continual refreshment from a stream so near the fountain head — so pure, so sweet a stream! CW IIIb, 2.

122. Look up to the blue heavens and love Him. CW II, 660.

123. Look well to our long, long, dear Eternity – in all things here only for His glory. CW II, 590.

124. Love makes labor easy. CW I, 87.

125. Mary, full of grace, Mother of Jesus. O we love and honor our Jesus when we love and honor her, truest proof of our blessed Church, the one our Jesus best loves. Mary, returning our love to Jesus for us. Our prayer through her heart with reflected love and excellence as from the heart of a friend, all delights us. Jesus, delighting to receive our love, embellished and purified through the heart of Mary. How unhappy they who deprive themselves of such happiness. CW III, 463.

126. May His dear sheltering wing be over you through all the storms. And when your dear wearied heart sinks and does not feel the immediate influence, then though hidden, He is nearest. CW I, 526.

127. May You enjoy true peace in Him who has nailed us, that Your little poor Mother does. I would not pull the smallest nail out for a thousand worlds. CW II, 682.

128. My daily object is to... take every event gently and quietly and oppose [present] good nature and cheerfulness to every contradiction. CW I, 480.

129. My dear one, your poor Mother looks only at Souls. I see neither American or English, but souls redeemed, and lost. ... Love your country yet also all countries. CW II, 306.

130. My faithful God, my heaven — my eternity — and so soon it may open to me. CW IIIb, 76.

131. My food is sweetened with the thought that I do my part to obtain it, and love and gratitude to Him who has ordered it so. CW I, 399.

132. My God, so good, and infinitely merciful — an eternity of praise will be too short, my God! CW IIIb, 76.

133. My Jesus first called me from nothing, drew me in pity to Him, loved me first, with an eternal love, and then called me to love Him, gave Himself for me, after I had become the slave of sin, bled and died for me upon the cross, after being a little Infant for me in the manger. And now with more than a mother's love, my Jesus, You bid me come and be fed and nourished even with Your own sacred flesh, Your blood, soul and divinity. Well indeed, may I fear to approach unworthily to such a Savior. CW IIIa, 264.

134. My Jesus, Savior, hide me. Shelter me; shelter the shuddering, trembling soul that lays itself in Your hand. CW I, 477.

135. My Savior! The triumph [joy] of my soul is with Saint Thomas, that You are my Lord and My God. I cannot touch Your sacred wounds as he did, but I earnestly desire with him to repair the faults and lament the sins which gave sharpness to the nails and spear that opened Your sacred wounds. You are my witness how truly my soul with all its power cries to You, my Lord and my God, whom alone I desire to contemplate forever. CW IIIa, 211.

136. My soul is sorrowful, my spirit weighed down even to the dust, cannot utter one word to You, my Heavenly Father. But still it seeks its only refuge and low, at Your feet waits its deliverance. In Your good time, when it shall please the Lord, then will my bonds be loosed and my soul be set at liberty. CW IIIa, 25.

137. Never let it enter your mind that you cannot be good in the station you are placed in. On the contrary, that is the very place God has appointed, and a performance of the duties of it would insure your salvation. CW I, 400.

138. Never mind, God is God in it all. If you are to do His work, the strength will be given. [It is] no great affair where His dear Atom is, if only His will be done. CW II, 506.

139. Not to moralize or repine, but in the common language of every day and hour, what is life except we consider it a passage and are therefore indifferent to the accommodations or casualties that happen in the dear, the strong and anxious hope of soon reaching our happy, heavenly home where peace and all we prize most awaits our arrival. CW I, 145.

140. Now our love so cold. Our Communions so cold! Bid Him call to the heavenly banquet; call us to love better in our Eternal bliss with Him. CW IIIa, 315.

141. O Jesus, with whom I offer myself, give me the courage to reckon myself as nothing, and leave nothing in me of self. You were redeemed with two pigeons, nevertheless, You suffered the sacrifice of the cross. Thus, Lord, all the exterior things that I may offer You not being able to redeem me, I must give myself wholly, and die naked upon the cross. I must lose myself in You. No more self, no more interest, but that of God. CW IIIa, 215.

142. O my God! We are the Daughters of Charity —from our happy solitude we look with desolation to the misery of the souls at large, we know how many do not know You, do not serve You. Our name devotes us to their service in any manner that we could truly serve them. We must bring them to the knowledge of and the practice of Your holy religion, to the habits of a good life. We must display for them the tender compassion of Your goodness, be the ministers of Your providence for the relief

of their miseries, a relief which disposes so well every heart to your better service – We must be a shining and brightening light of edification to all. CW IIIa, 319.

143. O my God, I am seized with terror at the view of the miserable condition of my soul, while still in its sins and exposed to Your eternal displeasure. I feel the earnest desire to make my peace with You and fulfill all the conditions which Your mercy has proposed to me. I will go to the feet of Your minister in all the sincerity and simplicity of my heart. I know [that] to confess to them my sins is to confess them to You. CW IIIa, 304.

144. O, my heavenly Father, I know that these contradictory events are permitted and guided by Your wisdom which only is light. We are in darkness, and must be thankful that our knowledge is not wanted to perfect Your work. CW I, 271.

145. O, whatever is Your good pleasure, Your blessed will be done! Let me have only one wish, that of pleasing You, but one fear – that of offending You, remembering the comparison

of my own unworthiness with Your goodness. Let my soul wait with patience and glorify You for Your patience with me. CW IIIa, 25.

146. Often, then must we say with Saint Ignatius, Lord, hide me in Your wounds till the storm of sin and death is over. O divine Savior, I know I deserve all the severity of Your justice, but if You would even now pursue me with it, You shall find me nowhere but in Your own Sacred Heart which was pierced and opened by Your love for poor sinners [who] have no strength, no hope, no refuge, but in Your bleeding wounds. CW IIIa, 210.

147. O my Blessed Mother, obtain from Him what is necessary for our coming to Him. That we may one day possess Him with you – for Eternity. CW I, 449.

148. Oh! How sweet to be every moment employed in the service and in the sight of the dearest and most generous of Masters who repays with the tenderness of compassionate love, even the good will of His child, however imperfect its execution. CW II, 28.

149. Oh my soul, who can measure our loss through the dissipation and negligence of our past life, like those unhappy persons who could have gathered treasures of merits, but go before God empty handed, or have nothing to present to Him but useless regrets and remorse for a barren and fruitless life. CW IIIa, 410.

150. Oh if all goes well for me, what will I not do for you, you will see, but alas, yet if I am not one of his Elect it is I only to be blamed, and when going down I must still lift the hands to the very last look in praise and gratitude for what he has done to save me — What more could he have done?"— that thought stops all. CW II, 606.

151. Oh, my soul, when our corrupted nature overpowers, when we are sick of ourselves, weakened on all sides, discouraged with repeated lapses, wearied with sin and sorrow, we gently, sweetly lay the whole account at His feet, reconciled and encouraged by His appointed representative. Yet, trembling and conscious of our imperfect dispositions, we are no longer the same. CW I, 479.

152. Oh, the holy and powerful petitions made for us on the altar! See my soul, the lifted chalice, the chalice of His blood. How great is our happiness in such a Savior! Can we be too confident in our petitions when we ask through His Blood and tears and sorrows? CW IIIa, 270.

153. Oh, well may I love God! Well may my whole soul strive to please Him. For what but the song of an Angel can ever express what He has done and is constantly doing for me. While I live, while I have my being in time and through eternity, let me sing praises to God. CWI, 265.

154. Our God, and He alone, will balance [all]. CW II, 405.

155. Our Jesus has triumphed over death for us, and softened all its terrors. Let us then think of our own passion and agony and death as our Jesus did of His, since with Him also we can say that a few days after [death] even our body will be restored to us – and our soul may be called immediately above. Perhaps, indeed, it may stop in purgatory, but its eternity remains secured. CW IIIa, 209.

156. Our look of love at Him draws back a look of love on us, and His divine look enkindles that fire of love in us which makes us remember Him continually. CW IIIa, 401.

157. Our Lord tells us to pray continually. This is not as difficult as you imagine. You pray with your memory when you remember God. You pray with your mind when you think of Him. You pray with your heart when you love Him. You pray with your lips when you speak of Him, and with your hands when you do your actions for Him and in His divine presence. CW IIIa, 387.

158. Our misery is not to conform ourselves to the intentions of God as to the manner in which He will be glorified. What pleases Him does not please us. He wills us to enter in the way of suffering, and we desire to enter in action. We desire to give rather than to receive and do not purely seek His will. CW IIIb, 109.

159. Our risen and glorified Savior would yet preserve the scar of His sacred wounds as bright and shining marks... of His victory over sin, death and hell, O divine Savior, show then these adorable wounds to Your Father for us. CW IIIa, 209.

160. Perseverance is a great grace. To go on gaining and advancing every day, we must be resolute, and bear and suffer what our blessed forerunners did. Which of them gained heaven without a combat? CW IIIa, 261.

161. Poor little I. Rich little I. Let the worst and worst that can happen, come... All is in the hands of [God] who gives. CW II, 201.

162. Poverty and sorrow — well, with God's blessing you too shall be changed into dearest friends. CW I 308.

163. Praise be [to] You, our Almighty conqueror, our heavenly Guide, our Friend, our sure and firm support, our light, our life, King of Glory, Lord of Hosts, adored, blessed. Praised be Your Holy Name forever! CW IIIa, 27.

164. Preserve me but this heavenly peace, continue to me this privilege beyond all mortal computation, of resting in You and adoring You my Father — Friend — and never failing Support. For this alone I implore. Let all other concerns with their consequences be entirely and wholly submitted to You. CW IIIa, 18.

165. Providence has disposed for me a plan after my own heart. CW II, 59.

166. Rejoice in Hope. It will all pass. How many pains are gone — and the joy to come is eternal. There we will adore and bless Him for having here numbered us with His own children. CW I, 533.

167. Remember the sure, the never-failing Protector we have, but He will not divide [share] your confidence, rely solely on Him. CW I, 72

168. Say often to God with your whole heart, Lord, I am not my own, I am all yours, I offer you my whole life and being. CW IIIa, 528.

169. Seriously, Eternity – it is such a long, long, day, make ready – CW, 484.

170. So far [as] I can express, to speak the joy of my soul at the prospect of being able to assist the poor, visit the sick, comfort the sorrowful, clothe little innocents, and teach them to love God. CW II, 62.

171. Surely the next blessing in our future existence to that of being near the source of Perfection, will be the enjoyment of each other's society [company], without dread of interruption from evil. No separation, but free communication of affection unshackled by the whys and wherefores of this world. CW I, 49.

172. Take the abundant, sweet, heavenly grace from day-to-day, only seeking and seeing Him in all our little duties, (so small an offering) and taking from the hands of all around us every daily cross and trial as if He gave it Himself. CW II, 600.

173. The best means to increase the love of God in our heart, which would make the practice of the presence of God so easy to us, is to consider Him as our tender Father – the Father from whom we proceed, in whom we live, – whose goodness and providence cherishes and preserves us through every moment of our life... Our look of love at Him, draws back a look of love on us, and His divine look enkindles that fire of love in us which makes us remember Him continually. CW IIIa, 401.

174. The fall of Saint Peter was indeed deplorable, but the sincerity of his repentance and penance will be our instruction to the end of time. Compassionate Redeemer, give one look on my heart, and give it this sorrow for my sins to go with me to my grave. CW IIIa, 204.

175. (Her thoughts on receiving the Body of Christ for the first time) The first thought I remember, was, "let God arise let His enemies be scattered," for it seemed to me my King had come to take His throne, and instead of the humble tender welcome I had expected to give Him, it was but a triumph of joy and gladness that the deliverer was come, and my defense and shield and strength and salvation made mine for this world and the next. CW I, 377.

176. The heart, down, discouraged at the constant failure in good resolutions, so soon disturbed by trifles, so little interior recollection, and forgetfulness of His constant presence. So many Communions and confessions with so little fruit often suggest the idea of lessening them, to fly from the fountain while in danger of dying with thirst. But in a moment, He lifts up the soul from the dust. CW I, 474.

177. The little daily lesson, to keep soberly and quietly in His presence, trying to turn every little action on His will, and to praise and love through cloud or sunshine, is all my care and study. CW II, 614.

178. The protecting Presence and consoling Grace of my Redeemer and God has never left me. CW I, 280.

179. The same God who fed so many thousands with the little barley loves and little fishes, multiplying them, of course, in the hands which distributed them. The thought stops not a moment for me. I look straight at my God and see nothing is so hard to believe in it, since it is He who does it. CW I, 370.

180. The service of God consists in the exercise of Faith, Hope and Charity. Do we give Him the service of Faith in applying to our spiritual duties; in improving instructions; in preparing for the Sacraments; confiding in His grace and assistance in our spiritual and temporal wants as a child trusts to its tender Father? Do we look at the trials He sends us with the eyes of our faith, seeing in our weakness and repugnancies our true penance and using

them as means of expiating our sins? CW IIIa,331.

181. The thirst and longing of my soul is fixed on the cross alone. CW II, 53.

182. The wintry storms of time shall be over and the unclouded spring enjoyed forever. So you see... with God for our portion there is no prison in high walls and bolts. No sorrow in the soul that waits on Him though beset with present cares and gloomy prospects. For this freedom I can never be sufficiently thankful. CW I, 265.

183. There is a Providence which never slumbers or sleeps. CW I, 9.

184. There is every hope that it [the community of Sisters] is the seed of an immensity of future good. CW II, 128.

185. They are passed away, I shall pass away. Neither one or the other is out of the order of God's Providence. CW II, 53.

186. Think often of your happiness. God destines you a share in His beatitude. CW IIIa, 526.

187. The charity of our Blessed Lord in the course of His ministry had three distinct qualities which should be the model of our conduct. It was gentle, benevolent and universal. Its gentleness appeared in His exterior manner and in His forbearance and moderation in all things. For what had He not to endure from the grossness and ignorance of those whom He taught His divine truths! With what condescension he managed their opposite [resisting] spirits and accommodated Himself to persuade and gain them. To how many rebukes and contradictions did He submit without complaining! CW IIIa, 193.

188. This morning at Communion, submitting all my desires and actions in entire abandonment to God's will. CW II, 52.

189. Tho' I sincerely love and respect individuals of other Faith, yet the Faith of the Catholic Church is the only one I can teach or advise to anyone committed to my charge. CW II, 638.

190. Thus, He might well say to us "Come learn of me for I am meek and lowly of heart", and at the same time know how much we ought to be so. Have I been as my blessed Lord? Have I learned to bear the weakness of others? They are obliged to bear with mine. Is it now unreasonable that I should require from them indulgence for the many faults that escape me and yet be unwilling to allow them their faults? The bad qualities of others should perfect and purify my charity rather than weaken it. CW IIIa, 508.

191. Time shall be no more, Eternity reigns, an Eternity of endless days, endless ages. Time, division of time no more. My God how awful [awe inspiring] this thought. All I know is there will be no more of such time as is now my own. CW IIIa, 508.

192. Tribulation is my element, if only it carries me home at last, never mind the present. CW II, 94.

193. Truly I feel all the powers of my soul held fast by Him who came with so much majesty to take possession of this little poor Kingdom. CW I, 377.

194. Trust all to our God as I must and do. CW II, 514.

195. Upon my word, it is very pleasant to have the name of being persecuted, and yet enjoy the sweetest of favors. To be poor and wretched, and yet be rich and happy. Neglected and forsaken, yet cherished, and most tenderly indulged by God's most favored servants, and friends. If now your sister did not wear her most cheerful and contented countenance, she would be indeed a hypocrite. CW I, 431.

196. We are followers of Christ, and every action of our life should be done in union with Him, since from Him only they can draw either value or merit. CW IIIa, 506.

197. We are like helpless destitute children who can do nothing, have nothing and must perish if left to ourselves; but by the invention of the infinite love of our Jesus, He unites us with Himself and makes us a part of Himself both in soul and body, so that we may have recourse to Him, as to a tender parent; we can lay at the foot of His altar every affection, every desire of our heart approaching Communion. He is all goodness. What may we not hope if we are only faithful to our grace! CW IIIa, 269.

198. We have the best ingredients of happiness — order, peace and solitude. CW II, 82.

199. We honor [Mary] continually with our Jesus — His nine months in her. What passed between them? She alone knowing Him, His only tabernacle. CW IIIa, 463.

200. We may be sure that our Savior offers Himself for each one of us every time we offer our full soul and body there with Him. CW IIIb, 71.

201. We must be so careful to meet our grace. If mine depended on going to a place to which I had the most dreadful aversion, in that place there is a store of grace waiting for me. CW II, 595.

202. We must walk, and walk confidently in the obscurity of Faith. CW IIIa, 475.

203. We will be [in any case] under the refuge of the Most High, and glad indeed would I be, if I could inspire your dear soul with as much indifference as is in mine, provided His adorable will be done during the few remaining days of my tiresome journey, which being made with so many tears and sown so

thick with crosses, will certainly be concluded with joy and crowned with eternal rest– Look up, the highest there, were the lowest here, and coveted most the poverty and humility which accompanied their and our Master every step of His suffering life. CW II, 156.

204. We will praise — even now we delight to praise the excellence we see. We call for the praise of all creatures, of all creation! And our Jesus took on Himself our humanity as if to unite all material creation to the spiritual, to give praise to His Father. CW IIIa, 314.

205. What are our real trials? By what name shall we call them? One cuts herself out a cross of pride; another, one of causeless discontent; another, one of restless impatience or peevish fretfulness. But is the whole any better than children's play if looked at with the common eye of faith? Yet we know certainly that our God calls us to a holy life, that He gives us every grace, every abundant grace; and though we are so weak of ourselves, this grace is able to carry us through every obstacle and difficulty. CW IIIa, 262.

206. What can a creature so poor in resources do? I must trust all to Divine Providence. CW II, 19.

207. What is the universe to us? Jesus, our all, is ours, and will be ours forever. And yet, we are not our own but His to whom He has committed us. O happy bondage! Sweet servitude of love, absorb, control, and pacify. Look up my soul, fear not, the love which nourishes us is as unchangeable as Him from whom it proceeds. It will remain when every other sentiment will vanish. And could we desire more than to draw continual refreshment from a stream so near the fountain head — so pure, so sweet a stream! CW IIIb, 2.

208. What should be the nature of our first intention in order that it may sanctify our action? First, it must be to please God and for Him as its principal object and end. It must also extend to every action of life ... We need not renew our intention in every action, but must watch not to retract our first morning offering or to turn willfully from our first great end proposed, namely, to please God. CW IIIa, 410.

209. When I lay my sorrows at the foot of the cross, it seems to me they vanish before so great an object, or become endeared by a participation with Him Who was sorrowful unto death for me. So the thought of His mercies and tender providence make me ashamed of my little griefs and ingratitude for His goodness. Oh, my God, I dare hope to find You, even at my last hour and judgement, what You have been to me through life. CW IIIa, 501.

210. When I see these souls die without Sacraments, without prayers, and left in their last moments to the conflicts of parting nature without the divine consolations which our Almighty God has so mercifully provided for us, I feel then, while my heart is filled with sorrow for them, as if my joy is too great to be expressed at the idea of the different prospect I have before me in that hour through the divine goodness and mercy. CW I, 385.

211. When so rich a harvest is before us, why do we not gather it? All is in our own hands if we will but use it. CW IIIa:258.

212. When will you reign with power and peace within? When will you rule, with absolute sway, over my whole life and being? CW IIIa, 449.

213. Whenever the Evil has most force, He [God] throws the veil of peace over the soul that confides in Him. CW I, 47.

214. Whether it is His pleasure to advance or retard my views, His dear blessed will be done. I have none. But if He continues to give me Himself, I am blind to everything I else. CW II, 47.

215. While my sins crucified my Savior, He was asking pardon for them, and His very blood was my peace. Now, then, heavenly Father, look down upon our altar. It is the same compassionate Savior who prays for us now as He prayed for us on the Cross. CW IIIa, 269.

216. Who are we to praise You? But we call on all Your creation to praise You! The birds of the air, the inhabitants of the earth, and the depths of the sea, the mountains and the valleys and whatever You have made to praise, to bless, to declare Your glory. CW IIIa, 310.

217. Who can resist? All self must be killed and destroyed by this artillery of love — one, one, one, one. Who could escape this bond of unity, peace and love? O my soul, be fastened link by link, strong as death, iron, and hell as says the sacred Word. CW IIIb, 109.

218. With what grateful and unspeakable joy and reverence I adore the daily renewed virtue of that Word by which we possess Him in our blessed Mass and Communion. CW I, 378.

219. Yes, my soul, the moment approaches, the supreme moment of life; our King comes; our merciful, compassionate Jesus, the King of Glory, the God of our hearts and our portion forever. He comes not with His thousand thousands attending, but in sweet gentle smiles of peace. He waits in silence at our door. No pomp of majesty presses round Him, but clothed in the humble veils of His love, He seeks only the repose of a pure and faithful heart. Give me, Your heart, my child, He says, it is all I ask. My King, my God, enter in mine, humble and poor indeed, but earnestly desirous of pleasing You. CW IIIa, 274.

220. You are a child of Eternity. Your immortal crown awaits you and the best of fathers waits there to reward your duty and love. You may sow here indeed in tears, but you may be sure there to reap in joy. CW IIIa, 262.

221. You have put a new song in my mouth, the song of salvation to my God. O, order my goings in Your way that my footsteps slip not. If the empty vessel is best fitted for Your grace, O, my divine Redeemer, what did You find to obstruct Your entrance in my free heart, set free in the liberty of Your children? This day You have entered in, and having sent before Your own benediction, it was waiting for its Master with many signs of longing desire. Did anything else possess it? Not even a remnant of human affection, not a thought or a wish which did not speak Jesus. CW I, 473.

222. You know I always look directly upwards. CW II, 138.

223. You know my corruption and excessive weakness. Destroy my corruption, strengthen my weakness that I may so really renounce my sins and my bad inclinations as to be truly purified of all the stains which now disgrace my

soul, O my God, redeemed by the blood of Your Son, Jesus, my gracious Savior. Amen. CW IIIa, 295.

224. You know that the peace and confidence of the soul in her Creator must be her true happiness and the end for which it was created. To enjoy we must love, and to love we must sacrifice. CW II, 161.

225. You must take courage with me, and push on, and do not let your mind rest on the sad thought of future prospects since the providence of God turns out so often quite different from our calculations. CW II, 460.

General Subject Index by Quotation Number

1. Catholic Church 75, 80, 95, 120, 189

2. Charity 20, 30, 41

3. Confession/Penance 143, 151, 181

4. Courage 12, 13, 14, 209

5. Cross 89, 127, 133, 141, 172, 215

6. Death 9, 13, 20, 49, 65, 112, 155, 185, 191

7. Eternity (Heaven) 9, 31, 32, 50, 68,82, 85, 92, 93, 99, 107, 112, 123, 130, 139, 150, 169, 171, 191

8. Eucharist, Communion 13, 74, 80, 89, 116, 133, 140, 175, 179, 188, 210, 218, 219

9. Faith 3, 13, 23, 35, 51, 53, 55, 64, 70, 114, 122, 126, 160, 176, 178, 180, 202, 206,

10. God, Father 8, 10, 11, 14, 17, 19, 23, 36, 39, 41, 42, 43, 45, 46, 47, 53, 54, 57, 58, 68, 79, 83, 94, 100, 101, 104, 118, 130, 136, 153, 156, 167, 173, 220, 222

11. Grace 52, 172, 201

12. Holy Spirit 56, 118

13. Hope 62, 63, 82, 105, 166

14. Jesus Christ 22, 59, 66, 74, 97, 106, 113, 115, 119, 120, 127, 133, 134, 141, 146, 155, 159, 187, 190, 193, 196, 197, 204, 207, 209

15. Mary 18, 19, 48, 108, 111, 125, 147

16. Mass 19, 34, 66, 152, 215, 218, 219, 200, 221

17. Mercy 69, 104, 117, 132

18. Peace 25, 54, 67, 77, 127, 152, 164, 213, 224,

19. Poor, Poverty 65, 161, 162, 170

20. Praise, Prayer 2, 4, 5, 6, 16, 17, 18, 33, 123, 132, 150, 153,157, 163, 204, 221

21. Sin, (Forgiveness) 8, 28, 69, 74, 88, 102, 135, 136, 149, 151, 174, 223

22. Suffering 85,86, 87, 103, 109, 110, 117, 126,136,139, 143,158, 182, 192, 203, 205, 209,

23. Will of God 7, 20, 27, 58, 60, 61, 70, 77, 81, 84, 91, 113, 137, 138, 144, 145, 158, 161,165, 168, 177, 183, 203, 208, 212, 214

Notes